Thrive

Summer Outdoor Nature Activities
For Children and Families

The Early Years
2 - 8 years

Gillian Powell M.Ed.

D1464694

Copyright 2021 © Gillian Powell

Acknowledgements

Thank you to my husband Tom.

Thank you also to Steve, Dave, Mary, Suzanne, Antony, Philip, Lisa, Conor and Leah.

To Darragh, Dylan and Sophie,and all the little people who made this project special and to all the children and families who have inspired me over the years.

To my wonderful colleagues in early years education, may they be blessed and of course to my wider family and friends.

A special thanks to Liz Casey who gave guidance at all times and of course to Orla Kelly publications who made this a lovely experience.

"Come away, O human child to the waters and the wild,
To the waters and the wild
With a faery, hand in hand".

W. B. Yeats

Contents

Introduction   1

Healthy Eating   18

Creative Activities   25

Sensory Walks in the forest   25

Fairies   26

Mathematical Concepts   39

Wild Things   39

Create a hideout   43

Magic Pencils Secret Codes   44

Maths Activities   55

Pulleys and Balance   59

Science Activities   64

Mathematical Concepts   74

Well Being Activities   81

Climbing in the woods   82

Emotional Well Being Activities   84

Introduction

The story of the outdoors in summer is one of abundance and joy. It is a time of freedom for children, a time where play can be the thing. Play allows children to "wallow in their learning and reflect on it" (Bruce, 2004). In a world where self-reflection is in short supply, playing in the forest is a great place to start.

In our Spring edition I highlighted how outdoor and nature experiences can benefit children. This is reinforced by research.

Playing outside, children benefit from being exposed to sunlight, natural elements and open air (Bilton, 2010). Richard Louv, the author of eight books about the importance of nature for children and families, says that children who play outside are "less likely to be sick, to be stressed or become aggressive and are more adaptable to life's unpredictable turns".

In fact, play is so important for children's development that it is recognised in the United Nations Convention on the rights of the child (Article 31).

I believe that summer is a time of abundance and imagination. This summer edition of Thrive will explore nature and outdoor activities that will develop children's cognitive and creative thinking. These activities have been tried and tested over thirty-two years working in an early years setting. The underlying principles of this book reinforce the importance of nature for children and families.

Thrive continues to emphasise mindfulness and holistic emotional well being, for children and families.

Yeat's poem is an invitation to go outside to the waters and the wild. This booklet will encourage you to stay there and explore a world where your child can develop cognitively. However, more than that children can connect with you and develop physically and emotionally and become healthy well-balanced adults.

So step outside in summer, feel the grass, swim in the streams, follow the butterflies and listen to the gentle breeze.

"The chance to connect with the natural world: first hand experiences of life and growth: endless opportunities for creativity and imagination: improved fitness and physical development – the countless benefits of outdoor play have a real positive impact on children's lives." - Into the Woods Outdoor Nursery U.K.

I would add to that, the chance for families to connect with each other, making memories that last a life time.

References

Barnardos (M.Willoughby), 2014, *Outdoor Play Matters* resources@barnardos.ie

Bruce Tina, (2007, 4th edition) *Developing Learning in Early Childhood* Sage Publications, U.K.

Bilton H.,(1998) *Outdoor Play in the Early Years: Management and Innovation*, London :David Fulton.

Louv R., (2013). *Last Child in the Woods*, Atlantic Books, U.S.A

What you need

- ☑ Comfortable clothes and a change of clothes.

- ☑ Waterproof coat – fleece-lined in cold weather.

- ☑ Waterproof pull-ups (fleece-lined), if it is cold.

- ☑ Wellies

- ☑ Healthy snacks are necessary for any trip with children.

- ☑ Fruit and a sandwich.

- ☑ Drink – Water

- ☑ A flask of tea and a snack for the adults is always a welcome treat.

- ☑ Treasure bag – A special bag to collect the treasures of the walk

- ☑ Knapsack.

Remember the following

Be safe

Run free and have adventures, but make sure you take care.

Leave no trace.

Be considerate of places and other people.

Engage Your Senses

Summer in the woods

Sight

In summer it is all about the light, and there is a myriad of different tones and colours to see all around you.

Prompt questions for children

- Can you see the sparkle of sunlight through the leaves?
- Can you see the sunlight dancing on the water?

- Can you see butterflies, ladybirds or other insects?
- Look to the sky (Be careful not to look straight at the sun).
- What can you see?
- Look at the eyeline, what can you see?
- Can you see flowers?
- What colour are they?
- Notice the colour, shape and size of everything.

Child with nature's butterfly wings

What you need

Cardboard.

A scissors.

Masking tape or glue.

Natural materials.

Directions

Cut out a butterfly, using a Stanley knife or sharp scissors. Use soft wool to loosely tie the wings around your child's shoulders. Use masking tape or glue to stick on the flowers and leaves of your choice.

Sound

Prompt questions for children

Take a moment to breathe, can you hear the breeze?

Can you hear the stream?

Sight

Can you see the reflection of the trees in the river?

Can you see your own reflection?

Smell

Outside in summer is full of smells, the scent of honey-suckle or elderflowers.

You can make elderflower cordial.

The elder flower is a tree with magical and medicinal properties. In folklore, it was thought to ward off evil and has been used in natural medicines over many years. It is also a delicious drink.

Be careful to positively identify elderflower as there are poisonous lookalikes.

Elderflower cordial

What you need

A cooker and adult supervision.

2 litres of water.

4-6 unwaxed lemons.

1kg sugar.

20 elder flowers, the creamiest, freshest blossoms, (no stalks).

A sieve.

Extra water to dilute.

Directions

Bring the water to the boil.(Note: supervise carefully).

Add the chopped lemons, elderflowers and sugar.

Place a lid on the pan and simmer for 30 minutes. Leave overnight.

Pour the mixture through a sieve.

Serve diluted with water for a refreshing drink.

Touch

There are so many things to touch in the woods in summer, but the most vitalising sensation is to paddle in a forest stream.

The cold, the sense of life, and the pure fun of splashing in a forest stream has to be the essence of the outdoors in summer.

Taste

(1)Picnics

Summer is a time for picnics, but it can also be the time for encouraging children to eat more fruit and vegetables.

(2)Blackberries and sunshine

Perhaps you can do some blackberry picking. Nothing tastes better.

(3)Nature Summer Scavenger Hunt

Find a seed or a nut.

Find some moss.

Look for all the colours of the rainbow.

Red – leaf orange – butterfly yellow – leaf green – fern blue – sky indigo – flower violet – petal.

Find something taller than you.

Spot a cloud shaped like an animal.

Find 5 of the same thing.

Find something that snaps.

Find something that feels cold.

Healthy Eating

In a Health Behaviour study in school-aged children in Ireland, it was found that only one in four children in Ireland eat fruit and vegetables every day.

Summer is a great time to get children eating more fruit and vegetables.

It is important to give children agency over what they eat, perhaps you can grow some vegetables.

Summer is all about the picnic, and families can encourage children to eat healthily by packing something fun.

It is important to encourage children to help you shop and prepare healthy food. Children can help with chopping and creating all of these fun snacks.

The first thing to bring is a flask of tea or coffee for the adults.

Peanut Butter Butterfly Sandwiches

What you need

Good quality bread.

Peanut butter.

Tomato.

Peas in a pod.

Snails with celery, apple and cucumber

What you need

Peanut Butter.

Cucumber slices.

Apple.

Celery.

Hummus Bear Face

What you need

Rice Cakes.

Hummus.

Apple.

Cucumber.

Raisins.

Cheese and cracker pizzas

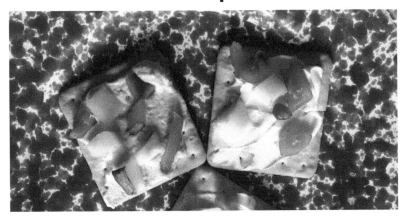

What you need

Crackers.

Grated cheese.

Tomatoes.

Cucumber.

Red peppers.

Banana Rainbow

What you need

Bananas.

Cream cheese.

Chopped fruit.

An orange – Rainbow with sunshine.

The picnic is ready so it is off to the forest.

Lady Bird strawberries

Strawberries.

Blueberries.

Cream cheese and raisins.

Teddy Bear Treats

You can bring the ingredients and cut the fresh fruit in the woods.

Children love to design their own face.

Talk about the designs, the shapes, the eyes, ears, nose, and smiles.

Watermelon Popsicles

Creative Activities

Creativity is the freest form of self-expression. It allows children to express and experience their feelings. Creativity also fosters cognitive growth. The process of creativity is the important thing and that process has two key ingredients; exposure to a wide variety of experiences and allowing children to follow their interests.

Sensory Walks in the Forest

Sensory Walks - Prompt questions for children

Can you hear something?

What can you feel?

Touch the soft moss, crack a twig, notice each sensation.

Fairies

Fairies and folklore have been part of all cultures for millennia, and they have long captured the imagination of children, all be it, half excited, half scared. In our local forest, there is a fairy trail, but follow your child's creative ingenuity and create your own fairy trail.

Fairy Doors

The entrance to the magic world.

A lucky black cat.

Fairy Trails

Fairy doors can range from the simple to more elaborate.

A simple fairy trail could involve collecting special leaves or stones and painting them.

A selection of fairy doors

Fairy Doors

Design your own fairy door

Pastel chalks are suitable for taking to the forest as they are effective and easy to carry.

You can do more elaborate designs at home.

What you need

Card.

Scissors.

Door or any shaped pieces of wood.

Directions

Cut out a fairy door from wood or card and decorate as desired.

(1)Fairy Doors with Foam

(2)Fairy dresses

Children can create their own fairy clothes with leaves and wild flowers and leave them on the trail for the fairies.

(3)Fairy Flowers

What you need

Scissors, paper or card, masking tape.

Directions

Encourage your children to draw a picture of a boy or girl.

Fairy Dresses

Encourage all shapes and sizes and all children's efforts.

Cut it out.

Attach masking tape.

Design your own dresses.

(4)Fairy Clothes Line

(5)Fairy Houses

Children love to build and there is nothing more engaging than building little rooms for the fairies.

Of course, fairies love a nice garden.

You can be creative and elaborate.

(6) Fairy Gardens

(7) Fairy Food

(8) Fairy Wands
What you need
Wool and sticks.

No fairy house would be complete without a fairy wand.

These can be made simply with sticks, but you can also decorate the wands with natural materials and old bits of wool.

Let your imagination run wild. These are two examples of wands made simply with glue and pastels.

(9) Fairy Spells
Suggestions for spells
A spell for peace and love in the world.

A spell to keep you safe and healthy.

A spell to keep the earth clean.

Extended learning
This is the type of play where you can engage with your child and be a co-constructor in their imagination. You can develop their vocabulary by talking about the rooms and everything that's needed- walls, ceilings, and more complex concepts such as how will you cook?

Prompt questions for children
Do your fairies have a name?

What is their favourite thing to eat?

Tell me about their family?

What do they like to do every day?

Would you like to leave a message for the fairy?

Mark making, just scribbling on the ground with a stick or on a page with a pencil is a lovely way to connect here.

(10) Message in a bottle for the fairies

I pretend the fairies speak to me, and my messages are important life messages, e.g. the fairies say to take care of the woods.

Mathematical Concepts

Mathematical concepts such as big, bigger, biggest, long, longer, longest and small smaller, smallest can be explored in this type of play.

Wild Things

There is a wild creature in all of us and in it is our most precious nature. In his beautiful book, *The Boy, the Mole, the Fox and the Horse*, Charlie Mackesy asks:

"What is that over there?" It's the wild, don't fear it".

We all have a wild nature and some children need to embrace their wildness and their imagination. There are some children with a wild rambunctiousness to them and they find solace in the wild creatures.

You can create wild creatures everywhere and the first thing a wild creature needs is a hide out.

Can you find a wild thing?
Look out for wild creatures in the shapes around you.

This wild thing has a huge mouth.

A wild thing in the ground.

The eye has it, a wild thing watches over the river.

Literature

WHERE THE WILD THINGS ARE, Story and Pictures by Maurice Sendak. (2001), Penguin, London.

This is an engaging child's book about a little boy who conquers his fear of the wild things and realises that home is where someone loves him best of all.

President Barack and Michelle Obama perform a beautiful reading of WHERE THE WILD THINGS ARE at The Whitehouse on April 25th 2011, (available on YouTube).

Create a hideout

There is often a natural shelter area in the forest, but you can have hours of fun carrying logs and branches to the side of a tree to make a hideout.

You can also bring Action men, Paw Patrol or Beanie Boos to the forest and create small hideouts for them.

Prompt questions for children

Would you like to live here?

Who would live here?

How would you keep out the rain?

What would you sleep on?

Compare your home to this hide out?

Magic Pencils Secret Codes

All children love secret codes and magic pencils

What you need

Magic Pencil

A feather, a pencil-sized stick, or an old pencil from home.

Blackberry Ink

Ink - Adult supervision necessary

Half a cup of blackberries.

½ a teaspoon vinegar and a pinch of salt to preserve the mixture).

Saucepans.

Boil vigorously.

If this is too much trouble just bring a small bottle of paint to the forest.

Magic Paper
What you need

A cold tea bag and sheets of paper.

Directions
Magic codes need magic paper. This is really easy to make with a cold tea bag. Let the page dry and you have authentic spell paper.

Invisible Ink

What you need

2 tablespoons of baking soda.

1 cup of water.

Cotton buds.

Paper.

Juice/or very watery paint.

Directions

Dip the cotton bud into the invisible ink mixture and write a message on your paper.

Let the paper dry completely.

To make the message reappear, dip a cotton bud in a cup of juice or watery paint and rub it over your message. Hold it up to the light to see the message clearly.

A secret happy message

Prompt questions for children
Listen to your children's messages.

This is the time to listen and I hope you are amazed by what you hear.

Extended Learning

Make a trail – follow the signs

This is an example of a simple trail following blue blocks of wood on the path. The two tasks are to find a fairy door with a shamrock and to find a "magic" tree stump.

Magic Paper made with a teabag

To create a treasure map effect just dab a tea bag on the page and let it dry.

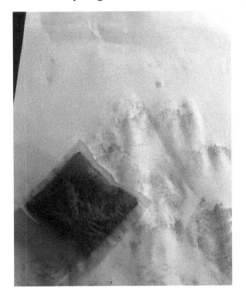

Follow the trail

Find the fairy door with a shamrock and find the magic tree stump. Follow the blue log trail.

A blue painted wood circle marks the trail. They should be easy to see and placed at regular intervals. Follow the blue painted circles.

Trail Markers

An owl marker

An acorn marker – Can you find an acorn?

Go to the large tree stump.

Follow the arrows.

Children can easily make their own trail with arrows or stones. Collect some white stones or sticks and plan a trail. Here are some examples.

Follow the 1 white stone trail.

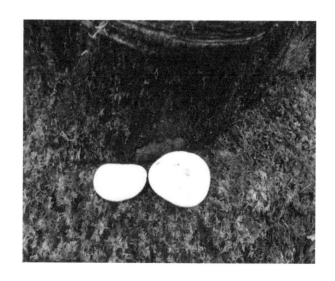

Follow the 2 white stone trail.

Follow the sticks with string ....

Maths Activities
Balance

This stream has a wonderful balance log.

Children can use their thinking and physical skills to solve problems. Balance is an example of this. If you watch your children crossing a stream, they will quickly decide which is the best stone to balance on. They will take risks but they will instinctively know where to put their feet.

The importance of risk taking -

The same applies to climbing. As children explore, they need an environment that engages them. They learn to trust their bodies to guide them. Children repeat the behaviour to allow themselves to develop their skills. They also repeat the behaviour because it is fun, but it also develops a child's sensory integration.

Balance stones to create a tower

Children can explore the size of stones and categorize shapes and size.

Find a climbing tree

Children learn about spatial relations and this helps children to understand how objects relate to each other (Daly, & Beloglovsky, 2016).

Spend some time crossing the stream and climbing trees. The child will reinforce their learning with every experience. Children can explore the concept of balance by walking on a log.

"Children may fall and will get bruises because that is part of learning"
Marjorie Ouvry, Education Consultant and Author

Capacity

Children love water and summer is the perfect time to play with water. Two simple containers can keep children engaged for a long time. They can collect and transfer water and stones and in the process children can develop their gross motor and fine motor skills. Pouring and transferring water and stones is an effective way to develop hand-eye coordination. (Daly & Beloglovsky, 2016).

Pulleys and Balance

2 red buckets on a rope in a pulley system

Prompt Questions

Which one is the heaviest?

Take some water out. What happens?

Language Development

Children can explore the mathematical concepts of capacity, beginning with the simple concepts of empty and full.

Children can also explore the concept of small, big and biggest in a game called "Who can make the biggest splash?"

Extended Learning – Capacity

Explore the concept of half full, half empty, heavy and light.

Extended Learning – Pulleys

For extended learning pulleys develop mathematical skills. Create a pulley system with a rope over a tree and ask your child to climb as you hold the rope.

You can also create a pulley and tie a bucket or different coloured buckets on to a piece of rope and explore capacity.

Children love to fill and empty buckets, three buckets in a stream can provide hours of fun.

A full 2 litre bottle – (included is a little natural blackberry dye for photographic purposes).

Half Full – Use a measuring jug for extended learning about milli litres and litres.

Can you fill a bucket to the top?
Can you fill a bucket half full?

Science Activities

The basis of science is observation and over the years I have seen children spend hours watching snails, ladybirds, and butterflies.

Snails

(1) A snail in hand

Fun facts about snails

Snails carry their home or shell on their back. This shell stays with them for life.

Snails have a top speed of 45 metres per hour. That is 3 school buses end to end.

Snails are the slowest creatures on earth.

They eat leaves and stems of flowers and crops so they are a gardener's pest!

As they move along, they leave behind a trail of mucous. This means they can stick to a surface so they can move upside down.

Snails are deaf, but they have 2 pairs of feelers which allow them to smell and feel.

Snails are nocturnal, so they like to come out at night.

Snails hibernate in winter.

Snails live up to 20 years.

Prompt questions for children

Can you walk faster than a snail in an hour?

(2) Snail poem

Slowly, slowly, very slowly,
Creeps the garden snail,
Slowly, slowly, very slowly, leaves a silver trail.

(Trace your fingers up your arm).

Quickly, quickly, very quickly,

Runs the little mouse,

Quickly quickly, very quickly, round the house.

Race your fingers up your arm

Language

Reinforces the concepts of fast and slow.

(3) Snail Creative Activities

Create spirals outdoors with different natural materials.

Snail art, Mandala art

Flower art

Snail trails in the garden
Find 2 snails and watch how far they move
in an hour, an afternoon, a day.

A snail foot

A collection of snails. (The correct term is a rout or a walk of snails).

Lady birds

The gentle touch of a ladybird.

Compare a ladybird to the size of a drop of rain water.

Fun facts about lady birds

They can fly.

Some lady birds are called after the number of spots they have, i.e. 4 spot, 7 spot.

They love to eat tiny bugs, lots of them, they can eat 5,000 in a lifetime.

They love warm weather and get active when the temperature reaches 16 °Celsius.

They know when the bugs are no longer around that winter is coming and they hibernate for the winter.

They can make sticky feet which taste yucky to anything that wants to eat a lady bird.

Lady Bird Life Cycle Song

(To the Tune of The Wheels on the bus)

The ladybird starts out as an egg,

As an egg, as an egg.

The ladybird starts out as an egg, clinging to a leaf.

The egg hatches into a larva, larva, larva.

The egg hatches into a larva.

That sheds skin many times.

The larva becomes a pupa, pupa, pupa.

The larva becomes a pupa, that attaches to a leaf.

Inside the pupa a ladybird is formed, ladybird is formed, ladybird is formed.

Inside the pupa a ladybird is formed.

Until it's ready to crawl out.

Patterns

Creative activities
A pastel coloured ladybird
Find a stone, paint it red with natural paint or bring a pastel or outdoor chalk to the woods.

Find a natural dark circle to create the spots.

Mathematical Concepts

Counting spots on the lady bird.

Ladybirds have the same number of spots on each wing, this is an example of symmetry. One side is the same as the other.

Can you find other examples of symmetry outside? For example a leaf.

A lady bird can have an odd spot which spans both wings.

Extended Learning

What the Ladybird Heard by Julia Donaldson and Lydia Monks.

This is a witty adventure about the silent lady bird and all the things she heard.

Listening Activity
Take a deep breath, count to 4, breathe out and listen.

How many birds can you hear?

Can you hear any animals?

What can you hear?

Literature
We're Going on a Bear Hunt by Michael Rosen and Helen Oxenbury.

This is a classic, and can really be enjoyed in so many ways.

Activities
A bear hunt in the forest
What you need
A teddy bear and an adult with a good memory.

Directions
Hide the bear or let a child hide the bear and play hide and seek.

Mathematical Concepts
Counting Bear, Bear can count trees, big trees, little trees.

Bear could count, leaves and sticks and stones.

Teddy Bears Picnic
Bear sandwiches.

Food could include something long and wavy like long slices of celery or cucumber.

A deep cold river i.e. a drink of water, Something squishy, such as hummus.

Create a cave and hide a treat in it. See healthy eating ideas p18-24.

Act out the story
Children love sound effects and this simple book has it all. It also serves to explain very important concepts.

Concepts to explore
On, Over, Under, Through, Round it.

A big one, deep, cold, scared, dark, swirling, whirling, narrow, gloomy.

In my experience children love to act out the story of We're going on a Bear Hunt with sound effects.

Lots of hand gestures are required, see the beautiful illustrations in the book.

For example

Uh-Uh a river!

A deep cold river. – Shiver

We can't go over it. – Hands Up

We can't go under it. – Kneel down, hands down.

Oh no! We've got to go through it!

Splash Slposh! Splash Splosh! Splash Splosh!

The children love to stamp and shout – Splash Splosh!

This builds a sense of rhyme and encourages the exploration of the sounds and meanings of words. This is so important in language development and pre-reading skills.

Extended Learning
Make a bear hunt map
See page 50.

What you need
Treasure paper with an old tea bag (see page 46).

Draw a simple map and follow the trail.

Extended Learning

To extend learning find something beginning with a letter sound.

Find something beginning with "s".

Well Being Activities

In research, movement has been identified as the most crucial mode of learning for young children (Bilton, 2010:13). Gallahue observes that success in motor skills can improve self-image (Gallahue, 1989).

There are many opportunities to move in the forest and also to experience risky play. The Department for Education and Skills of the U.K. in a 2007 policy document states that through risks children can learn from their mistakes. (DfES, 2007:8).

There is no better way to build risks into play than climbing trees.

References

Bilton, H. (2010) *Outdoor Learning in the Early Years Management and Innovation.* Oxon, U.K, Routledge.

(DfES) Department of Education and Skills (2007) *The Early Years Foundation Stage.* Annesley: DfES publications. U.K.

Gallahue, D. (1989) 2nd Edition *Understanding Motor Development: Infants, Children and Adolescents.* Benchmark Press, Virginia, U.S.A.

Climbing in the woods

Go slowly, build children's confidence and stick to the lowest branches for a while, it will not take long for your child to become competent at climbing.

Climbing Fun

Emotional Well Being Activities

Sweet Spot – Mindfulness activity

In the spring edition we learned about the sit spot, where a child finds a spot in the forest and sits there, counting to 4 on the in-breath and out-breath. Meditating, this takes meditating to a sweet spot level.

Find a sit spot, take a deep breath and close your eyes (if the child is comfortable with that).

Breathe out and count to 4 as you do, now think of something nice you did, or something that makes you happy and remember how you felt.

Directions you can give to the child:

Were you smiling?

What were you doing with your hands ?

Were you moving?

Think of this happy memory and breathe

in, count to 4, breathe out, count to 4.
(Courtesy of Dr. Roberta Hines and Dr. Sarah Cassidy, ACT course 2020).

Mindfulness Activities for children and adults

It is time to leave the woods, sit in a sit spot, breathe in and count to 4 as you breathe in, breathe out, and count to 4 as you do.

From your sit spot, reach out your hand, feel the ground, feel the moss, the leaves, the bark of a tree.

Feel your own hands.

Gently massage your own hands.

In this moment of gentleness and gratitude, be grateful for you.

Dear Reader,

If you enjoyed this book, would you kindly post a short review on Amazon or Goodreads? Your feedback will make all the difference to getting the word out about this book.

To leave a review, go to Amazon and find the book. Then scroll to the bottom of the page to where it says 'Write a Review' and submit your review. Thank you in advance.

If you enjoyed this book, you might also like other books in the Thrive series: Spring - Autumn - Winter collection for the Early years (2 to 8 years).

Lightning Source UK Ltd.
Milton Keynes UK
UKHW021501300521
384591UK00007B/91